APPROACHING THE FIELDS

APPROACHING THE FIELDS

POEMS

CHANDA FELDMAN

LOUISIANA STATE UNIVERSITY PRESS

BATON ROUGE

Published by Louisiana State University Press
Copyright © 2018 by Chanda Feldman
All rights reserved
Manufactured in the United States of America
LSU Press Paperback Original
FIRST PRINTING

DESIGNER: *Mandy McDonald Scallan*
TYPEFACE: *Apollo MT, text; Burford, display*
PRINTER AND BINDER: *LSI*

Library of Congress Cataloging-in-Publication Data

Names: Feldman, Chanda, 1976– author.
Title: Approaching the fields : poems / Chanda Feldman.
Description: Baton Rouge : Louisiana State University Press, [2018] |
    Includes bibliographical references.
Identifiers: LCCN 2017037452| ISBN 978-0-8071-6829-5 (pbk. : alk.
    paper) | ISBN 978-0-8071-6830-1 (pdf) | ISBN 978-0-8071-6831-8 (epub)
Classification: LCC PS3606.E3857 A6 2018 | DDC 811/.6—dc23
LC record available at https://lccn.loc.gov/2017037452

FOR MY PARENTS

AND FOR MORRI

CONTENTS

CONTENTS

THREE

FOUR

ONE

NATIVE

Forget kudzu, that closed weave,
its green congesting trees, the way it twins

a telephone line's length with vine, its only message
to overrun.

Forget the river's muscled sweep
where nothing intrudes

and stays the same, water changing
what it washes through—retooled

stone, redrafted bank. Forget the difference
between foreign and native. Anything

can take hold here and spread. Indiscriminate
landscape. Even the road flinches

alive—a snake whips dust and slinks to a ditch.
Air's adaptive, lifts whatever needs flight:

spore or song. The day's margins blur
dark and light. Forget the dead

stay down, they persist as haints. A murky story
sticks to any relationship:

beloved or despised. A confederation
binds enemy and alliance, just as

the ground takes us in
and decay makes us kin.

3

BLOOD

Rivulets down
the generations. The lineage
of crippling

bunions, gap between
the front teeth, firecracker fits—
all the things I hate

about me. Murmured
from body to body, a hushed
murderer's tributary, Great-great

Uncle Red, rust-briar bearded,
leveling a gun at another man.
Maybe all hearsay.

It's not in the blood anyway,
but wound deeper down. Messages
hammered into cells. My father,

the first degrees in the family—
night lab work, tissue details
under microscopes. He photographed

me on Ivy League campuses
to make them my history.
Bloodlines no longer

the full story. We never knew
what dammed in my mother.
Her body without warning

quit flushing its toxins. Traits
I'd be tested for—the factors
that overflowed.

SETTLE

We were in a place we rarely go
anymore, the door key in my mother's purse,
as if her childhood house had options, wasn't its own

dead end. The cocklebur- and ragweed-choked
yard. The windows busted through, someone had dragged
the couch into the driveway, a few plates brimmed

with rainwater. It was never much
to begin with. A shotgun house on cinderblocks,
plumbing never installed. The roof's tin lid,

wind-hooked, bent.
I'd always wondered what befell
those homesteads along highways. Slackened—

the crib barn's withered oak. How a family recedes
from the decline. Now I know
it can happen swift. The Mississippi River's ferry

service suspended. The lumber mill leaving
workers waiting in line. No one makes a living
farming these days. No one takes over

the uptown shops—all the undressed
window displays.
                        Staggering—

we were in a field I used to love and
hate. The thumbfat bees at the water-pump. Dogpacks
switching through goldenrod. The hill's stitched

in soy and cotton. The crying
panther I'd fear to hear before knowing
it was a tale. No one in the family could believe

my grandmother's request: to be buried between
her two late husbands. It had been thirty years since
their bones rose on floods and washed away.

Who would remind her
it would have to be otherwise? It just made sense
to let it go.

RIVER JUBILEE

After the spring rains' glut and drain—
the adults drove to the river with nets
and buckets tethered to pick-up beds.

At the docks they peeled off their socks,
unbuckled shoes. The men rolled up dungarees
and sleeves over the knobs of elbows and knees.

Women gathered dress hems into knots
above calves to keep their shifts from sipping
the current. Nothing to hurry: the fish

straggled in the shallows, coal-dust
catfish, striped bass, and the glass
of sunfish along the bank. A convergence—

men and women came twisting down woods-
trails from the bluff until river mud sucked
their feet. Nets swooshed over fish-bodies,

they'd twitch and writhe until slapped
into buckets, and still more, flip-flopping
in the shallows. The wet, mouthy odor

of water, river-grit spangling ankles. The adults
crooned *I'll be damned*'s, as they met the flesh
shouldered up on the waters.

BLACK-EYED SUSANS

In Tennessee, I spot them all over—
rimming ditches, clustered in understory.

Button faces obeying skyward,
floret-skirts breezed through, trembling.

Black-eyed Susans. What you pick to claim
who loves you and who loves you not.

First flowers trudging up June hills—
what my father calls nigger daisies.

Hard to forget how he's learned them—
cursed like a weed, too common

to be handsome. Their flagrant
canary rays swish around a head, blue-

black, violet and brown. It's a flower
that roots anywhere—in fields exposed

to blunt sun. Thriving despite
rocky soil, drought,

and threatens to overrun other
native plants. In a lifetime my father's

had to choose the boxes for himself
from Colored, Negro, Afro- and

African American, to Black. No one true
name for things. It was an Englishman

observing flora in the wilderness
that named the daisy—of the aster family,

Rudbeckia Hirta,—after a friend.
Nigger Daisy, Gloriosa, Indian Summer,

Yellow Girls, Black-eyed Susans,
among roadside rubble and dust,

grown up from disturbed lands.

ELECTION DAY

No one picked in the fields on Election Day—
The trucks drove us to a picnic on the Bluff.
The children sang songs like it was Sunday.
We ate salads, melons, and iced cakes.

The trucks drove us to a picnic on the Bluff.
We filled our plates from the barbecue drum.
We ate salads, melons, and iced cakes.
Cold drinks iced in a tub the size we bathed in.

We filled our plates from the barbecue drum.
Balloons bobbed in the air around us.
Cold drinks iced in a tub the size we bathed in.
The adults leaned on trees, kept to the shade.

Balloons bobbed in the air around us.
The children jumped rope, drew in the dust.
The adults leaned on trees, kept to the shade
When the midday beers were done.

The children jumped rope, drew in the dust,
The men, one by one, signed for their ballots.
When the midday beers were done,
Who knows where the votes went—

The men, one by one, signed for their ballots.
The man you sharecropped for chose your say.
No one picked in the fields on Election Day.
The children sang songs like it was Sunday.

PSALM

Louis Southworth, a slave and violin player
in the Goldrush.

Let's strum the old hymns, gather for prayer.
Song's a communion, the bread of prayer.

Keep me from the church where silence is
the measure. My violin's my mouth open in prayer.

My bow comes down soft and gentle-like
I forget the work and the years I've lived with prayer.

When my master worshipped the whip,
I thought death was my only mercy, my last prayer.

Maria, I wrung gold from water to pay
my cost—freedom, always my dearest prayer.

The most holy music I know, Maria,
the psalms of our bodies clasped in prayer.

Devotion has a choir of many tongues.
There are no wrong notes in prayer.

ELEGY

Gathered in the yard, shed-side, pokeweed,
black walnut, pecan tree, all leafed and
umbrellaing. My grandmother, the relatives

constellating after my grandfather's funeral
as the sons and grandsons spill their beer
and whiskey-on-the-rocks obeisance in the weeds

among my grandfather's metal underpinnings—
wheel axles, piled riggings, the teeth and claw
digging and rooting tools. The goings inside

for chicken and cake. My grandmother
won't sleep in her bed tonight, she'll stay
on her sewing room's single mattress, the walls'

peach, floral lace curtains, the black enamel
Singer's needle pierced mid-stitch in fabric.
After the burial, I sit at her sewing table

and roll off my nylon hose. In view
above, a photograph: my grandparents
and their children in front of their old house

and fields. The seven sisters aligned
on one side, the six brothers on the other,
a flock's V-flight, beside my grandparents.

My grandmother's apron over her dress,
her work interrupted for this. Beneath
my grandfather's straw brim, he's staring off

into his soy crop. For the final breaths,
my grandmother held my grandfather's hands
and wiped wet swabs over his lips.

Inside the photograph, inside their old house's
right angles and load-bearing beams, there
was a long table set with jarred peach preserves,

sorghum and pepper vinegar; there was
a maze of rooms, a new one added for each
two children born. That house burnt down

some time ago. I remember the late-night call—
nothing was saved, not even one spoon,
my grandfather saying gone is gone.

CENSUS

Their names are on record, 1930.
Pearl, William, Zanie, Kitty, Edna, Jessie,
my great-grandparents, another great-
grandfather, my grandmother, her two sons.

Pearl, William, Zanie, Kitty, Edna, Jessie,
living in a two-room house, a dirt floor,
my great-grandparents, my grandmother, her sons.
The questions posed at their door,

a two-room house, a dirt floor.
I listen for a chorus of *No's*
to the questions posed at their door,
the enumerator's looped cursive script.

I listen for a chorus of *No's*.
No one was able to read or write.
The enumerator's looped cursive script.
No one owned any of the property.

No one was able to read or write.
They were Negro, one mulatto.
No one owned any of the property.
A question mark follows a birthdate.

They were Negro, one mulatto.
My grandmother was born in Tennessee.
A question mark follows a birthdate.
My grandmother was twenty, approximately.

My grandmother was born in Tennessee.
All of their industries were cotton.
My grandmother's sons' were six and four.
All of their occupations were farmhand.

Their industry was cotton. My great-
grandparents, my grandmother, her young sons,
they all worked as farmhands.
Their names are on record, 1930.

INTERIOR

My grandmother's bedroom. The walls and ceiling—
she'd dipped a feather duster in black paint,

printed plumes. Two windows,
two beds, end to head. Blankets and quilts.

A little straw step stool, an iron stove.
My mother and grandmother once sat there

in facing chairs, in winter. I remember
watching them one moment as a child.

A carbon print writing pad in my mother's lap.
My mother wrote what my grandmother said.

My grandmother spoke toward a window—
the yard, the crop's leftover stalks

crosshatched in frost and mud rows.
Inside, what was said to be sent

passed through the air to my mother's
hand. My grandmother walked the field road

home to birth my mother in her room.
My mother slept there as a child in a bed

at her parents' feet. The floor's worn
wide-plank boards. The bureau's oblong

and oval mirror missing a piece. My mother
signed her mother's name to the letter.

TWO

TRUE AUTUMN

I return to the dead-end street
where I grew up, at the edge
of the county, at the foot of lavish
green hills, with dogwood- and magnolia-
plotted medians, where once a year,
my mother places a two-gallon bucket
of chitlins straight from the deepfreeze
next to the stove's warmth to thaw.
The long chain, slime-gray,
lovingly scrubbed clean of grit.
My mother says it's not true autumn
without eating them, as vital as blood-
rich colored oak leaves. As a kid
I loved the slurp of entrails
slicking my throat, but I never forgot
my white neighborhood friend's table
set with bowls of lobster bisque
and baguette slices. Contained. Not all
food-juice mixing on the plate.
Over dinner my mother talked stories
of her father stringing hogs
for November slaughter as segue
to discussing black family mobility,
and my father drew imaginary lines
from stomach to mouth, a knife gutting
the hog body. How quickly matter
comes apart, as with words, how
to convey my family's two-acre lot
where we feast on saucy delicacies
while trading superstitions about haints
and spirits and, in the next breath,
discussing protons penetrating solids.

How I used to crave no barrier
between me and other families. I'd pass
through brick and into beige safety—
no jellied pig's feet, no hot combs
smarting the ear, no smell of oozing
chitlins when it's near winter and
too cold to throw open windows
as we did, each time we filled the house
with their sweet stench.

1976

In their first fall, married, living
in graduate student housing,

Taliva Court, Knoxville, Tennessee.
The bed made with their wedding quilt:

rose pinwheels, stitched helixes
coiled like vines among flowers.

Their first car they name Nova Jean.
My mother drops my father off

at the research lab. She takes classes
in the Home Economics building.

My mother in turtleneck, cameo locket,
her curls teased into an Afro.

A plaid blanket spread out beneath
their picnic in the Smoky Mountains:

seafood salad, chocolate pie, and cola.
They bought shrimp for weeks

after their first time ever eating it.
The way my father holds my mother—

his camera timer set—they're in a grove,
the light spindles, the fall foliage begins

to turn on the limestone lookout;
against the peaks, small waterfalls seam

the mossed stones. In this time,
before they're my parents, they're in love

with a first child, the one in the womb
whose heartbeat won't be picked up

in the final week of the third month.
It matters most my father and mother

hold each other again and again,
before they begin their days

on those cold mornings
of tears that lead them to me.

IN THE MIRROR

Mornings my father wiped a circle clean in the mirror steam,
a towel wrapped around his waist, his face lathered
with a pale gold powder mix from his porcelain mug.

A shaving blade scraping against his jaw, then dipped
in the sink. His wax kit and scissors laid out for his mustache.
Some mornings, I rummaged in his closet, past the suits,

the camouflage vest—its elastic slots for rifle shells,
his army jacket, a dashiki, for the checkered shirts my mother sewed
for him long ago. On the floor were his racked shoes

that I polished, the bag of toothbrushes and cotton cloths
I used for buffing between the stitches of his Johnston & Murphy's.
Whenever he was fitted for a suit, I accompanied him,

examined his sleeve, the subtle woven colors
in the wool's weave as my father stood in the triple mirror,
its infinite reflections of him. I wore his old ties

with ankle-length skirts and combat boots. I watched
as he wrapped a half Windsor knot and slipped it
over my head, cinched it closed at my neck. After school,

I stacked cordwood beside him in the yard, worked
the weed whacker, the chainsaw, and he let me sip
from his double shot of Jack. Chamber music on the stereo,

we'd grill in the backyard, sit through dusk's mosquitoes,
fireflies, June bugs, and moths. I didn't know my own
strength, my father said to convince me my hands

were as good as his—that time passing me the garden hoe
to cut a chicken snake sprawled on the warm floor
of our garage—that I was the best son or daughter he could have.

DEMONSTRATION

At the county extension service in the old downtown,
I spent after-school hours in my mother's office—
the green-glass building next to the city farmers' market

held in the parking lot each week—the entrance lined
with dark-stained oak cabinets, quarts
of tomatoes, the perfectly suspended fruit-flesh

in red liquid. Men holding Chinese food cartons
of soil, like purses, from their gardens and farms.
The soil needing to be fixed, the levels adjusted,

they'd puzzle over results laid out like blueprints.
My mother, a home economics agent, working
upstairs in the demonstration hall and kitchen,

the double-burner stove tops, the steaming silver pots.
In her hairnet, a lab coat over her blazer and
satin blouse. I sat in the chairs for the audience

with my homework until she called me up
to the platform to dip pH sticks to read the acid
contents. I'd slip the skin off peaches, level tablespoons

of salt for brines. My mother taught me
each step: the maceration, the strawberry-rhubarb
slurry heating to frothing, the sugar thermometer

rising to the gelling temperature of precisely 220
degrees. My mother pouring the fruit into scalded jars,
the room billowing with sweetness.

DANCE

I see myself turn on shuffle-ball-change
in the dance-room mirrors and back to center.
The night before I was up at Love Circle.

I dig my heel and step. I brush forward and back
warming up to dance. I stood in the grass

and had lain in the grass; houselights and car lights
down below us. Right then left, five, six, seven,
eight. My feet in black patent leather, bow-tied

black grosgrain. My tights and black leotard,
the only black clothes I'm allowed to own,

the color my mother says is for adults. Almost
dark, I had lain on the ground; the grass,
the leaves were dying back. My mother waiting

in the dance lounge, a magazine in her lap,
she eyes my moves. I hop from foot to foot;

I drop into a sweep and leap. Chimney smoke
was sweet from the houses in the cold air.
The flannel inside to his coat. Slide, stomp.

Sweat on my forehead, my back, my chest,
a damp scent. If my mother could look into

my head, which she couldn't. . . . Almost dark
and I had lain down at Love Circle. We left
the car and walked into the grass. I step-

ball-change back to center. Before the light died,
his blue eyes, each hair on his body red, rust

freckled bands over his skin. Were we back
before we were missed? I had lain down at Love
Circle, the grass, the leaves were dying back.

JUST WHEN I TRY TO OPEN THE DOOR

Sentences unravel like leaves
from limbs or a fraying hem. Winter

in the brain, all white space, erased terrain.
Each beginning frozen before it falls.

Or desperate gestures beckoning
semantic strangers who turn away

& language evaporates. I want to flee
like unbound geese, leaving

for southern climates where lexicon is
lush. Where X can attach to any green.

Yet how to describe the current
freeze. Dig out white words

in a white room &
what to make of suffering through.

MY FATHER STANDS AT THE MISSISSIPPI RIVER BRIDGE

Maybe the cold brought you
back, the snow clumped like fur

on your neck, or the radiance of ice
clinging to rocks along the narrow river.

Did you hear the steel grates creak,
the harsh wind cracking on the beams?

Whoever turned you away
from your private sorrow, it wasn't

your wife. She is on a train
watching the frozen white fields fly

backwards in the window, moving
toward you.

Did the water cramp
and roar from below? Were you thinking

of declarations: yes, no, never,
always, this is the last time.

Were you so sure there was nothing
worse than grief? You will ache

when your first child breaks from the birth
canal coiled in her mother's cord.

You will sit with your father
drinking bourbon by the woodstove.

His house will flame so bright after nightfall,
the rooster will crow.

Whatever made you choose to live
through this trouble, will place you

in desert cities. You will be lost
in another tongue by a salt-crusted sea.

You will never know the future,
so you can bear to go forward.

HEADWATERS

I've wanted to fall
           from the body like water.

I am a river,
rocks are memory: I turn them,

rub them until the rough rounds and is no longer
a sharp to carry.

                 You and me,
touch cuts
across years. I used to say I hate,

but the heart changes. Do you see how
my body dissolves? Your hands

spread like streams.
                 Love can be a steep rush—

it brings the heart's roar
      from source to mouth.

CUSTOM

My grandmother, who wanted to be buried
down home, wouldn't recognize the road:

New Highway 51 North, new Paper Mill,
new cemetery. Unsettled ground, we were told,

rain shifting the grave. My mom waited
as long as it took to cover her mother

with the first handful of dirt. In those parts,
it's a custom for drivers to pull aside

when the dead pass by. Men and women,
strangers, stepped from their cars, hands

over their hearts as the funeral procession
made its way. I cried with the first bitter blasts

of November weather that hit me, the sky's
perfect blue day after a week of rain.

Among the plates piled with food
in the church basement after the funeral,

I sat among my unknown relatives.
My mom, I'd not visited in over a year,

her slim brown hands, slicing the thinnest bite
of chicken. Her asking me for a paper napkin

in a soft drawl. I have to bury her one day
was there between us, her small helpings

she wasn't hungry for, her loss I couldn't ease.

APPROACHING THE FIELDS

We're so close that we can't not stop—fields,
late fall, days after the killing frost, and the cotton

ready for harvesting. The bolls shocked open—
unspool ripe cotton on the wind until we walk

into a blizzard of it. My mother wishing
her mother and aunts and uncles could look up

from the rows ahead at her and her sister,
picking. They called my mother *Coo* for slim-

beaked fingers pinching cotton from the boll
without getting pricked on the plant briars. Now,

the process is machined, spindle pickers reaping
eight rows at once, the bales, like loaves

of plenty, wait for a trip to the gins at the field's
ends. My mother's been trying to tell me

about where she's been. My mother, who crossed
the threshold of the afterlife, who died

her three minutes before her heartbeat was revived,
who came back with a sense that there was no

heaven's gate on the other side, not even
something like night, like quiet, that if she was

absorbed into anything, she was lost to its workings.

THREE

BUT WE LIVED

1. But We Lived

But we lived, my mother told me, day to
day. It always was and we never thought
it wouldn't be—separate entrances

at the doctor's, dentist, the fabric store, or
the places we knew not to go. The lines
and the laws and the signs, as you saw

in *Eyes on the Prize* on TV. When
the law changed—I had two cousins, they said,
y'all can go to the white school now, it's our

right. Twins. They signed up, they went.
Nobody minded them. They sat in class,
had lunch on the lawn. One full grade report—

the teachers flunked them in every subject.
After that they came back to the black school.

2. Sharecropping

The year ended at the black schools in March.
Children going to the fields with their parents.
My family sharecropped at the Hughes' place.

The Hughes owned the Movie Palace in town,
our little house. They had a pond our church
baptized in. I remember Mrs. Hughes

scolded my parents: *it's too cold in the fields*
for that child. Each morning I ate one runny egg
at a little pine table. The Hughes ate

at their dining table. It could be an hour or two,
I sat buttoned up in my coat, ready to go
as soon as they gave me permission to go.

3. Friday Night

My parents gave me permission to go
to the Ritz Movie Palace on Fridays.
First we frolicked at the café, no first,
we got fish filleted at the fish market.

You took it to the café and they fried it
with potato slices. Families ate early,
me with my mama and stepdaddy,
everybody in pressed dresses and slacks.

Later, the children went home, the adults
stayed, danced, drank. I still had to pay
for movies, but I didn't have to sit
in the colored gallery. We sharecropped

for the owners. I sat with the whites.
Everybody knew better than to complain.

4. Cutters' Fabric Store

My 4-H agent, Ms. Bernice, complained
uptown at Cutters' Fabric Store. Why
didn't they hire a black to serve their black
clientele? I was a high school senior and still

picking in the cotton fields. Ms. Bernice—
taught me to sew, lent me my first Singer—
got me the job. I greeted black women,
Hello, Mrs. —, ushered them to the new

stock. My boss liked the business I brought.
I became the first black in town to work
the cash register for blacks and whites. But
I hid the best bolts and notions for my women.

To shape a dress in their minds, I'd drape
and cinch a rich color over their shoulders.

5. Ceremony

I sewed my wedding dress in cameo white.
Your father rode the bus from the Massachusetts
military base two days before Christmas.
(His suit was his army green uniform and cap.)
We were married in the church—a first
in our community. Until that, we'd crowded
in the main room of somebody's little shack.
Bride and groom jumped the broomstick.

Your father and I on the altar steps,
white carnation bouquet, our parents beside us.
A photographer from the town newspaper,
The Leader, showed up at our ceremony, so
we have one picture of the event.

6. My Father's Father

Your granddaddy missed our wedding.
After fall harvest was weighed and sold,

your granddaddy rode four hundred miles
down to Louisiana. Stayed three months

as seasonal labor on the Mississippi levees.
My brothers and sisters and I did the rest

while he was gone, after school, before school,
cleaning the coop, slopping pigs, milking,

slaughter, chopping wood, hauling water
from the pump well down Starn's Hill,

near the turnoff for Richardson Landing.
That's where we met the ferry dropping off

our sugar, our corn coming back in meal sacks.
Did you know your great-great-grandmother,

a slave-chambermaid on the steamboats,
traveled this stretch of river back and forth?

7. My Father's Freshman Year

I traveled four hours by bus, two hundred miles
to the Black landgrant university from the bluff.

A knock, a fellow student's head inside the door,
and Dr. King was slain at the Lorraine. Night,

the Student Union Plaza, the sidewalks, into
the streets, the Black side of town:

Black medical school, Black private college,
the only Black-owned bank in the state

(where we held our first accounts). Then
a row ahead, a row behind, a row on either side,

the National Guard boxed us in, rolling us
back to the campuses. REPORT

TO YOUR RESIDENCE on the megaphone,
but not to our rooms, their rifles single-filed

us down into the dormitory basements.
A guardsman caught my eye as I took the steps.

I saw that he saw a situation with the equal
possibility of us alive and dead.

8. Laboring

Equally a place of living and dying—*shadow land,*
the midwives called the labor. An ax slid
under the mattress to break the bridle of pain;
two straight pins made a cross fastened to
the pillow warding off haints; the placenta
swaddled and buried deep in a yard grave. Gifts
of eggs and crackers for the new mother.
No one asked to hold the baby in the first six weeks.

The whole time the baby was arriving the midwife
talked under her breath, calling on God
to guide her steps, comforting with Bible passages.
They'd give you teas: tansy when things were lagging,
pepper to clear the afterbirth, and for a stillborn,
mint to keep the woman's milk from coming in.

9. Taint

The milk my mama and a neighbor drank
was tainted from a cow that must've ate
a noxious weed, but we didn't know that

at first. Her joints swelled, muscles seized,
fever, then her hair combed out in hanks.
Her teeth ached and she couldn't eat. We called

on the dentist—there was one white man and
his assistant uptown, their advertisement
painted on a building, $5 to pull a tooth.

With a toothache most black folks, even white,
couldn't afford more. The dentist set the clamp
and yanked out the problem. My mama's

beautiful, even teeth, but the pain wouldn't leave.
One by one, they pried them out of her mouth.

10. Baptism

One by one—they'd wade into the pond
we used as a baptismal pool in the side fields
where my family sharecropped. Our church
across the road, an old two-lane highway
dropping down from uptown to the river's
Chickasaw Bluff. As far as the road went—
sandbags, a sign said TERMINUS, for years
as far as I'd ever traveled.
                              A rerouted stream
fed the little pond. One by one, the minister
lowered the people beneath, raised them up,
drew away the handkerchief from their eyes.
The whole time watching, a few whites
staring down at us from the highway shoulder.

11. Choir

Above the highway, N. Main and Liberty, uptown,
a small community of blacks, our professional class,
teachers, ministers, funeral owners. My family lived

on the other side, the bottom dip on Loop Road.
The uptown houses, white cottages, green yards,
white lattice fences. Our shotgun houses scattered

and sunk among the crops. They had churches,
we had ours, but on Saturday nights, we met
for contests: male, female, junior, adult choir,

each time a different church, cookies and punch.
Mostly we won ribbons, our choir's name printed
in the local paper—one page for black community

news: school honor rolls, births, deaths,
marriages, our prayers for the sick and shut-in.

12. My Mother's Father

You had to be on your deathbed to stay in
from the fields, otherwise you went.

My daddy, one Friday night, shot
and killed a man. Sat in jail for two days.

Monday dawn the guard slides open the cell,
throws in a pair of daddy's work clothes.

The landowner in the car waiting to drive him.
My daddy never went back for a conviction—

killing a black man wasn't enough
to keep him from chopping cotton. Even now,

someone's son or daughter has a run-in
with the police, some black folk call on these

old connections, see if the white family
their families worked for can ease the sentencing.

13. On the Porch

Why she thought we'd ease her predicament—
spinning into the yard near midnight, waking
the house up, slumped onto her knees on our porch.
Her boyfriend in the driver's seat, high beams
trained on our door. The girl crying out
for my mother. This was the daughter of a family
mama cooked and cleaned for on occasion.
They lived in one of the South Main mansions.

How did she think we'd help? We said nothing.
We made no lights. Pretended a good night's
rest. The girl sounded like one of those panthers
the old folks talked about, claimed they yelped
like a crying woman. As a child, I didn't know
that was said to keep me clear of the woods.

14. My Father's Birthplace

Mama owned forty acres on the bluff,
inherited from her father, Sampson,
your great-grandfather. Two-hundred acres
divided among his five kids. His hands

built the church, the schoolhouse, planted
pecans up and down the road that bears
his name. It's said he came from Memphis
(too many lynchings). Originally arrived there

from somewhere in Virginia: a runaway slave,
unknown mother and father. Eighteen,
joined the Civil War colored infantry. Next thing
we know, he's seventy-five. Like a resurrection,

married your great-grandmother Katie, his
twenty-five-year-old bride. Ministering
his own congregation, farming his own ground,
no white people around, that's how they lived.

FOUR

PRIMING LIGHT

What I want is the assurance that when I go
I'll be taken to the hill. I can see it
In my mind, the grave they should walk me to.
It's almost land unknown, on the Tennessee-
Arkansas border, in woods above
The flood plain, where my ancestors are buried.
They never knew much of me; I'd be strange
To them, but if there's time for romance . . .
As if the day could be to scale. I imagine the dirt
Covering my body will be a good humus,
The loam of pin oaks and hickories. Leave me
With limestone markers for head and foot,
The ones that won't stand up to time,
My name's engraving left to erode under rain,
To be crept upon by moss. Leave me in the land
Of my priming light. O grandmother-cultivar,
Your roses beneath the kitchen windows. O
Fall men, your chests strung with the season's pelts,
Rabbits' blood in the sink. Let me retrieve
The yams, pull loose turnips from the garden.
Let me escape, O midday heat, to the north side
Of the house. Let me lie on my grandparents' bed,
Where their sex made thirteen children, let me
Sniff their scents there. I will die wanting
To hear again my name in the mouths
Of my old women. Let them call me in
My daydreams on the summer quilt to rise.

NOTES

"Native": After Kyle Dargan's poem "Quagmire."

"Settle": After Kate Daniels's poem "Crowns."

"Election Day": Despite the passage of the 15th Amendment to the Constitution in 1870, granting African American men the right to vote, and the 19th Amendment in 1920, granting women the right to vote, African American men and women in the South faced systemic voter intimidation and disenfranchisement, which spurred the passage of the 1965 Voting Rights Act.

"Psalm": Louis Southworth was born into slavery in Tennessee on July 4, 1830. In the 1850s, he accompanied his master to Oregon and worked mining gold and playing fiddle in California, Oregon, and Nevada. Eventually, Southworth was able to buy his freedom for one thousand dollars, and settled in Oregon. The poem's italics quote Southworth from the article "Church Cuts Darky Who Clings to Violin," *The Sunday Oregonian,* January 2, 1916.

"But We Lived" sequence: These poems are based on family stories during and immediately following Jim Crow–era segregation in the American South.

"1. But We Lived": In order to comply with the 1954 *Brown v. Board of Education* federal ruling to desegregate schools, Tennessee, among other states, allowed for voluntary desegregation. In Tennessee, some schools and school districts remained segregated until mandatory school desegregation was enforced through federal government lawsuits as late as 1971.

"2. Sharecropping": During the Jim Crow era, the academic year in black schools was commonly shortened so black children could work in the fields.

"7. My Father's Freshman Year": On April 4, 1968, the night of the assassination of Dr. Martin Luther King, Jr., and in the immediate days following, North Nashville saw civilian clashes with the city police and National Guard, including civilian rock throwing and gunfire. At Tennessee State University, a Black landgrant institution, the National Guard entered campus dormitories to search students and their rooms for weapons.

"8. Laboring": I consulted Kelena Reid Maxwell's Ph.D. dissertation, "Birth Behind the Veil: African American Midwives and Mothers in the Rural South, 1921–1962" (Rutgers, 2009) for this poem.

"14. My Father's Birthplace": Shelby County, Tennessee, where Memphis is located, had the highest number of recorded lynchings in the state of Tennessee during the mid-nineteenth century through early mid-twentieth century.

ACKNOWLEDGMENTS

Thank you to the editors of the following publications in which these poems first appeared, sometimes in different versions: *Alaska Quarterly Review:* "1976" and "But We Lived"; *arc journal:* "Dance"; *Cimarron Review:* "True Autumn"; *The Cincinnati Review:* "Interior"; *Ecotone:* "Priming Light"; *Flint Hills Review:* "Just When I Tried to Open the Door"; *The Journal:* "Psalm"; *New South:* "Approaching the Fields"; *Prairie Schooner:* "Black-eyed Susans," "Blood," and "River Jubilee"; *The Southern Review:* "Demonstration," "In the Mirror," "Native," and "Settle"; *Sou'Wester:* "My Father Stands at the Mississippi River Bridge"; *Spoon River Poetry Review,* "Headwaters"; *Torch Journal* (online): "Custom"; *The Virginia Quarterly Review:* "Election Day" and "Elegy."

"My Father Stands at the Mississippi River Bridge" also appeared in *The Ringing Ear: Anthology of Black Poets from the South,* University of Georgia Press, edited by Nikky Finney.

"Native" and "Settle" also appeared online in *Torch Journal* and on Verse Daily.

"River Jubilee" also appears as a free downloadable poster from Broadsided Press online at broadsidedpress.org.

"True Autumn" also appeared in *Gathering Ground: Cave Canem's 10th Anniversary Anthology,* University of Michigan Press, 2006, edited by Toi Derricotte, Cornelius Eady, and Camille T. Dungy, and in The *Ringing Ear: Anthology of Black Poets from the South,* University of Georgia Press, 2007, edited by Nikky Finney.

Thank you to the following institutions and organizations for generous support during the writing of this book: Bread Loaf Writers' Conference and the Bread Loaf Bakeless Camargo Residency Fellowship, the Cave Canem Foundation and community, Cité Internationale des Arts in Paris, the Community of Writers at Squaw Valley, the Djerassi Resident Artists Program, the Dorothy Sargent Rosenberg Memorial Fund, the Fine Arts Work Center in Provincetown summer workshops and the Walker Foundation, the MacDowell Colony, the National Endowment for the Arts, the Stanford University Wallace Stegner fellowship program, the Sustainable Arts Foundation, and the Vermont Studio Center and John Pavlis Fund.

Thank you to Dara Barnat, Nan Cohen, Jennifer Foerster, Judy Halebsky, Joshua Rivkin, and Metta Sáma for your close reading of versions of this manuscript, encouragement, and insight.

Thank you to Eavan Boland, Bill Brown, W. S. Di Piero, Ken Fields, Alice Fulton, Phyllis Janowitz, Ken McClane, and Natasha Trethewey for your teaching and example.

Thank you to Nicole Cooley for your confidence and support. Thank you to LSU Press, and especially MaryKatherine Callaway, M'Bilia Meekers, Erin Rolfs, and Lee C. Sioles

My deepest gratitude to my family. The completion of this book would not have been possible without your support and help: Troy Wakefield, Jr., Mary B. Wakefield, Marian Wakefield, Gerald Wakefield, Aspin Wakefield, Bill Feldman, Joyce Feldman, Morri Feldman, Jacob Feldman, Zachary Feldman, Noah Feldman, and Ella Feldman.

CPSIA information can be obtained
at www.ICGtesting.com
Printed in the USA
LVHW02s0020240118
563703LV00005B/469/P